100 Ways to
Love
Your Wife

A Life-Long Journey of
Learning to Love

By Matthew L. Jacobson

www.MatthewLJacobson.com

100 Ways to
Love
Your Wife

A Life-Long Journey of
Learning to Love

By Matthew L. Jacobson

www.MatthewLJacobson.com

*For my sons, that in striking blows in favor of civilization,
you might know and never forget how to love.*

100 Ways to
Love Your Wife

*T*his is a book of ideas – ideas that, if followed, will lead you toward an excellent marriage.

An excellent marriage . . . sounds good, doesn't it? It also sounds like an endangered species. Epic marriages are pretty rare these days, aren't they?

But, they don't have to be – not for you and me.

The best, richest marriages are enjoyed by couples of every age group who know a simple, yet all too often forgotten truth. Great marriages are the result of husbands and wives making a lot of everyday choices that say, *"I love you,"* rather than choices that say, *"I love me."*

If you want an epic marriage worthy of the best love poet, country western singer, playwright, novelist, or the Song of Solomon, then learn how to say, *"I love you"* through all the normal days of marriage that you are given.

That's the challenge, isn't it . . . all those days. They need to be filled with something, but most of us run out of ideas to keep marriage fresh. This book provides those ideas.

Not long into marriage, I discovered that just because I was satisfied and happy didn't mean Lisa was. I needed to learn and understand what every smart husband knows: Continually filling your wife's reservoir is an ongoing endeavor. But, doing so pays amazing dividends.

A loved woman – a cherished wife – is a giver, returning to her husband far more than he ever poured into her soul.

But, it doesn't happen all at once. If you take the simple steps outlined here and are consistent over time, you will enjoy a transformed marriage – a marriage transformed by love.

Life is short. Love her well.

"The two shall be one"

Genesis 2:24

He who loves his wife, loves himself

Ephosians 5:28

Introduction

I'll never forget those eyes, dancing above the rim of her glass the moment I walked into the room, the first dance of many . . . wild and wonderful.

As I lay across the bed from my beautiful, lovely Bride during our Hawaiian honeymoon (a typically generous gift from my brother and sister-in-law) those dancing eyes held my gaze, their radiance intensifying a vague sense of loss.

Time. Suddenly all those years without her seemed lost.

Drinking in the moment's wonder, my fingers fell lightly, high upon her cheek, tracing to her lips the soft outline of her face.

"Why didn't I meet you ten years ago? Where were you? Look how much time we've missed being together."

But life is like that, isn't it? One day we wake up in an oasis wondering why we wandered around in the desert for so long.

I purposed right then and there, 21 years ago, laying on the bed in our room on the 5th floor of the Lahaina Shores Hotel, on Maui, I would cherish this woman, my bride, this breath-taking gift from God, every day of my life.

How great it would be to report that I have loved Lisa perfectly. I cannot. I've caused her tears, been unloving, insensitive, and downright sinful at times. But, I can report to you that Lisa has been and is a cherished woman. I'll be transparent . . . she makes it easy for me.

I reach out from the inside to let her know how much she matters to me. She knows this – that it's serious business with me. Lisa is my priority because Jesus Christ made her my priority – and He expects to be obeyed. He wants me to love her as He loves His Bride.

Jesus is the example for every Christian man to know how to truly cherish his wife.

Wait a minute, Jesus isn't married!

But He is (or soon will be). His Bride is the Church.

And Christian men are instructed to love their wife as Jesus loves His – Ephesians 5:25

You see, if you claim to be a Christian man, being the husband of a cherished woman just isn't optional. It is the call of God on your life – to preach the Gospel with the power of your love for your wife – an expression to the world of how Jesus Christ loves His Bride, the Church. If Lisa isn't cherished, I'm walking in sin and I must change. The same is true of every married Christian man.

The Scriptures say, when you love your wife you are actually loving yourself . . . because according to God, the two of you are one single entity. And a truly cherished wife takes great pleasure in returning that love with interest.

What do you have to lose?

#1

She gave her heart to you. Value it for the sacred treasure it is.

ॐ ॐ

*E*very wife has a deep desire to be cherished – to be of supreme importance and value to her husband. If your wife's friends were asked the question about you, *"Does he cherish his wife?"* what would be the answer? Is the answer obvious to them? What would your own woman say? Does she feel cherished? To truly value her is to leave no doubt in anyone's mind, especially hers. Remind yourself often that you've been entrusted with something beautiful, something sacred. Then communicate to her that you know it, and that it matters to you.

#2

Reach for her often.

❦

*H*as it been more than one day since she felt your arms around her? As husbands, we get our needs met and then allow too much time to pass before we show affection through physical touch . . . meeting her needs. She loves to feel your arms around her, often. Do you have the kind of job that takes you away for extended periods of time? The importance of regular physical touch when you are present is even more crucial.

#3

After a busy week, run a hot bath ... just for her.

⧼⧽

*O*ccasionally slip unnoticed into your bathroom in the evening, run a hot bath with bath salts, light candles, turn on soothing music (or the things you know she'll like) and then tell her something is waiting for her in the master bath. Leave and lock the door behind you, making sure nothing will distract her for an hour as she spends the whole time thinking about how fantastic you are!

#4

Ask about her thoughts and her dreams.

☙ ❧

*I*nitiating a conversation that has your woman as its focus tells her heart that she matters to you, that you see her as an important person with her own ideas and dreams. In this way, she's no different than you. You want to be affirmed by being sought out as a person. So does she.

#5

Listen when she answers, not because you have to, but because the person you cherish is sharing her heart.

ೞ ೫

$\mathcal{L}$istening with interest says, *"I truly value and respect you."* What you hear are her words. What she hears in your understanding, engaged interest is a reassuring voice that says, *"I love you."*

#6

Romance her before, during, and after the wedding ... especially after the wedding, after the honeymoon, after the kids start to come and after they begin to head off to college.

⁓ ⁓

So many wives wish their men would desire to romance them – to do something that says, *"I'm thinking about you and want you to know how much I love you."* Sex may go a long way in saying "love" to you but it's only a small part of what says "love" to her. Don't stop loving her in non-sexual ways just because life got busy. Even when you're old together, she will never grow tired of being romanced by you.

#7

Buy her the best chocolate you can afford and keep her stash well stocked!

℆ ℅

At any given time, there might be approximately 4 married women on the planet who don't like chocolate. For the rest of you:

Step 1 – Find out what kind of chocolate she likes. Light, dark, truffles . . . get specific intelligence. It's important!

Step 2 – Leave chocolates on her pillow, leave them on the dresser, leave them conspicuously in the laundry room, leave them in her closet where she's sure to find them, leave them on her desk, at work. It's not really about the chocolate, it's about saying, *"I've been thinking about how to delight you, about how to make you smile."*

#8

Shower together every chance you get.

❧ ❧

*T*rust me, you just should.

#9

Tell her you really appreciate the dinner she made or that baking effort - every time.

❦ ❦

ove makes the simplest meal a feast. But if we're unwise with our words, we can turn a gourmet dinner into a famine of the soul. It's her heart on that table in front of you . . . remember, you care how she feels . . . you cherish her heart. Don't diminish her with a careless or snide remark, or with no remark at all. With the right perspective, and a wise, loving approach, even burnt casserole has its merits.

When she goes into that kitchen, she is making another attempt to say, *"I love you."* If something turns out as a total disaster, you can always and honestly say, *"I'm sorry it didn't turn out the way you hoped, but I appreciate so much the love that inspired you in the first place and I can live on that kind of love, forever."*

#10

Kiss every day but, more importantly,
kiss with passion - every time you kiss.

෴ ෴

A simple kiss on the cheek can be a throwaway gesture or an experience that contains the whole Book of Love.

#11

Send her away ... because you love her!

ॐ ॐ

She needs to relax and recharge, so from time-to-time send her somewhere away from the busy world you both inhabit.

She'll have so much more to give if you look after her needs in this way.

#12

Hold her close, until she feels the strength

of your conviction.

☙ ❧

Your wife has a heightened sense of the care you have for her. For the most part, she doesn't want a hug that says, "You're my pal." Husbands can communicate much with a hug so, don't give hugs that say, *"Whatever"*. She wants something more. Give the kind of hugs that say, *"I love you, a lot!"* When you hold her, make sure she knows where your true feelings lay. Make her a believer in the depth of your love with hands and arms that leave no questions.

#13

She's confusing you again, isn't she?

CR ♔ SO

Some women are better at this than others but the fact is, occasionally, our wives are going to send conflicting messages . . . conflicting to us, at least! To them it all makes perfect sense. Time to listen to Billy Joel's song, *Always a Women,* and remind yourself that she isn't a math equation – she's more like an Impressionist painting. Then smile and tell yourself how much you love her.

#14

You've removed your clothes but have you removed the obstacles?

CR ജ

She wants to be sexy with you so help her to be free and uninhibited by being the guardian of her privacy, her dignity, and her honor.

#15

Surprise her with a spontaneous "mini-date."

☙ ❧

*C*offee, smoothies, herbal tea, kombucha. Know what she likes, take her to that little hole-in-the wall café she loves, add conversation about the day, and suddenly you're having a date with your girl and she's feeling loved.

Wait a minute. You just spontaneously decided to go out for no particular reason and have a drink together . . . just because you like being with her?

You are making all of her friends jealous but that's okay. Keep up the good example to all the other husbands. They might take a hint. Marriages need a lot more husbands like you!

#16

Express thanks for the thankless jobs.

❦ ❧

When was the last time you vacuumed, folded towels, or mopped the floor? Some guys may respond, *"Oh, yeah, that's me!"* but for most, not so much. Notice and openly tell her how grateful you are that the laundry is done and the clothes are folded . . . again . . . and again . . . and again . . . (if you haven't been grateful, get grateful!)

Who doesn't appreciate their work being noticed? And, it's all the more meaningful when you notice it. She works hard, with much on her mind, managing, nurturing, loving, for most of which she rarely hears a "thank you". When she feels your appreciation, she feels loved, valued, and her spirit soars.

#17

Let her know you see her strengths, her unique gifts, and tell her that you value them.

❧ ❧

Your wife is a smart woman (she married you, after all, right?!). She could probably run a country. Build her up with positive words. It's as simple as offering praise openly, often, and sincerely.

You were amazing when you did that . . .

You are really good at . . .

I'm really impressed with your ability to . . .

#18

Make her your accountability partner.

CR SO

What could be easier than telling your guy friends all the ways you've failed when there's no possibility of rejection and they've fallen in all the same ways you have? Real accountability is about "not going there" - not about the fellowship of failure.

Allow no shadows in your relationship. Live honestly and tell her everything. There may be some pain at first but if you are humble and broken, it will make you stronger. If you've committed to face your wife in honesty and openness, suddenly being accountable has meaning and the path of shame and destruction doesn't look so good anymore.

#19

Tell her often, "You are so beautiful".

CR SO

Because she is . . . and she needs to hear you say it . . . because she forgets.

#20

Take her on a "housekeeping date" but don't tell her.

❦

*A*rrange for a housekeeper to come and clean your house while you and your Bride are enjoying a dinner out. You could hire a service or just involve some friends & family to come in and clean. Do you have older children? Ours are often in on the plan. What wife doesn't like coming home to a clean house, especially after a dinner out?

#21

When it comes to making love, gently ask
her what she likes.

◯3 ℰ◯

*T*hen follow through, with the goal of delighting her.

#22

*When it comes to making love, gently help
her understand what you like.*

ભ જ

*B*ut make sure she doesn't sense from you that she's
getting it wrong. Never, ever be critical or condemning.

#23

When it comes to making love, hold nothing back.

☙ ❧

*G*ive all of yourself — heart and soul, along with your body. Remember what the Good Book says: The two of you are 'one flesh' (Genesis 2:24).

When you find your dream girl, life is great.

We started out having coffee together every day at the local espresso place, down the street from our apartment. We only needed one chair. Or should I say, one chair and one lap. Trust me, it was *very* comfortable.

A few decades down the road and we're still at it – coffee together every morning.

I'm an early riser, which is perfect because I love making coffee for my woman (and, now my older daughters too). It's routine – the same every morning: grind the beans, put into the two French Presses just the right amount, skim the cream from the raw milk, get the bowl of raw sugar, find Lisa's porcelain cup with the little birds, and warm up my cup with hot water before the coffee is poured in. Then, I put it all on a tray and serve it to Lisa on our back porch (summer) or in the living room, near the fire (winter). I love serving her coffee, just the way she likes it.

Once in a while, when the roles are reversed, the same thing happens. My cup gets warmed up with boiling water because that's the way I like it . . . because she loves to serve me.

What if I didn't know she always prefers the porcelain cup with the little birds?

How could she know I want my cup warmed up before the coffee is poured in?

These things aren't "right" or "wrong" – just preferences – what we like.

A loving relationship is made up of delighting to serve your spouse – and so is lovemaking.

Wouldn't it be great to understand what your spouse prefers? What he doesn't like and what she finds appealing and relaxing. What she finds arousing, what turns him on? We don't know because we don't seek each other out. Because we don't ask. Because we don't talk.

This isn't hypothetical. Lisa and I have had this conversation. We're both glad we did and, so is God. When it comes to intimacy, He wrote the Book.

<u>Here are 5 things you can do to get the conversation going:</u>

1. Timing is important. Make sure you talk when your spouse can give full attention (no distractions and away from the kids!).

2. Choose a place. Pick a place where your spouse will be comfortable openly discussing details of your intimacy.

3. Make it special. It's a special conversation, so make the moment special. What does your spouse like? A quiet walk holding hands, or a dinner at a favorite restaurant, or sitting close on the couch?

4. Start the discussion focused on Her needs or His, depending on who is driving the discussion. The needs and desires of your spouse should always come first. It's always easier to listen *after* you've been heard.

5. Begin by saying something like this, "I've been thinking about our love making and I care a lot about delighting your heart, about pleasing you. Am I meeting your needs? How about your desires? What do I do that you like? Is there anything you'd like me to do that I'm not doing, or could do differently?"

When it comes to your turn to talk about what you need and like, be sure to start by being grateful for the things your spouse does that you like and appreciate – keep it positive.

Remember, romantic love-making is God's idea. He created you to delight in each other. It's easy to forget that the Song of Songs is in the Bible. You should read it sometime.

#24

Speak with gentleness.

☙ ❧

Y ou can make her hard and tough, but she didn't start out that way. She's a woman. She needs to be cared for. Care for her with the tone you use. Harshness will close her spirit toward you. Gentleness will open her spirit.

Pleasant words are as a honeycomb, sweet to the soul,
and health to the bones.

~ King Solomon, Proverbs 16:24 ~

#25

Accept that she thinks differently than you.

CR SO

*T*he wise husband doesn't want a "rubber stamp" wife, automatically validating everything he thinks and wants to do. She sees things differently and that is a very important benefit of her personality. Value it. Don't minimize her unique perspective and intuition – it's a God-given gift to help you make wiser decisions.

#26

When moments of frustration come, never forget ... What God has put together, let no man tear apart.

ᐊ ᐅ

*T*here's no getting around it, some moments in marriage are filled with frustration. When they come, never forget that God chose her for you and, even in the midst of frustration, you have something to learn: things like controlling your temper, like not giving full vent to your anger, like learning to listen, like not responding in kind, like listening, etc., etc.

A soft answer turns away fury but grievous words stir up anger.
~ King Solomon, Proverbs 15:1

#27

Seek her counsel.

କ୍ଷ ୫୦

Many wives say their husbands don't care about their opinion. Don't be that guy. It's not only foolish, it's wrong. The two of you are a single entity so, don't run off and act on the latest idea you and your buddies talked yourselves into. Be prudent. Seek her counsel.

#28

Listen to her wisdom after you've sought her counsel.

෴

So you asked her counsel, but did you truly listen? Many wives say their husbands never listen to them. Such a man is a fool. Instead, avail yourself of the wisdom and perspective that God blessed you with in your wife.

#29

When she returns from the salon, it's time for you to start talking.

⟮❧ ❧⟯

*C*ompliment her on her new haircut, or hair color, or hairstyle, or manicure, or whatever it was that she had done. Even though you've been married a while, she's never stopped enjoying that you notice her. It's just another way of telling her, *"You're my girl!"* And that *never* gets old.

#30

As a woman, she's always pouring out so, remember it's your job to always pour in.

❧ ❧

No woman remains fulfilled on great moments from the past. "Relationship" is always present tense. "Pouring in" simply means doing those things that make her feel loved and cherished.

#31

Notice that new outfit - she's dressing for you.

⋅⋅⋅

Don't let her arrive home in a new outfit from the store without telling her how great she looks. If it's still in the shopping bag just say, *"Hey, would you like to model that for me?"* and persist, even if she's shy about it. And, one more thing . . . remember, in these moments, she's not looking for your analysis or opinion, unless it along the lines of, *"You look amazing!"*

#32

Keep it frisky from the honeymoon to year 60 and beyond!

ೞ ೞ

*I*t's more fun that way and no matter how many years have passed, she still wants to be the object of your desire. There's not a single reason to let her pass you in the hall without giving her a playful _____. (You fill in the blank!) And besides, when the kids become teenagers, embarrassing them is a whole lot of fun, too!

#33

The Little Engine That Could needs a little rest.

CR ൭

Make sure your wife gets the regular rest she needs. She may keep chugging along like *The Little Engine That Could* but you know that without rest, she's going to crash. The fact is there are few priorities that can't wait until she's gotten proper rest. When it comes to her fatigue, be The Enforcer . . . she'll appreciate you for "giving her the permission to rest" and for creating the circumstances to make it happen. Besides, when her needs are met, she has more energy for all sorts of fun things!

#34

From the time they are very young, tell the kids how wonderful their mom is.

ജ ‍ ‍ ‍ ‍ ‍ ‍ ‍ ‍

*F*or wives and mothers, appreciation from the kids is like protein to muscles – it fills her with strength to meet the endless demands of her calling. And, you're meeting your responsibility by reinforcing what God wants them to do.

*~ Honor your father **and mother***

GOD, Commandment #5, Exodus 20

#35

Praise her to parents, family, and friends.

೦ಜ ೫೦

Look for opportunities to let everyone know how deeply you respect your wife and how proud of her you are. At some point, your third-hand compliments will get back to her . . . and, they will delight her heart.

#36

Never make negative comments, inferences or give disapproving vibes about your wife to anyone.

CR ♋ SO

*D*on't make the huge mistake of speaking negatively of your wife to others, and especially to extended family. As soon as everyone understands that the two of you are one, single, unassailable entity, they'll learn to respect her and she'll love you for it. Trust me – it makes for a secure woman and, a secure woman is a happy wife.

#37

Never put up with even slightly critical comments about your wife from anyone.

❦ ❧

*D*on't let the moment pass. Whenever something critical gets said, turn directly to the person and say, *"I don't appreciate that kind of comment about my wife."* Never leave any doubt where your loyalties lay.

#38

Admire her with your eyes.

CR ED

When you were dating and/or soon after the wedding, you were really good at this. There's no reason to stop now. In fact, now you have a lot more reasons!

#39

Admire her with your words.

☙ ❧

*D*on't let a day (that's right, not even one day) go by before you speak a positive, adoring word to her. If you're not present, use an email or a text, or a quick phone call. Even the simplest words of admiration (if sincere) will run deep . . . all the way to her heart.

#40

Banish sarcasm from your speech.

ல் ௯

Sarcasm might be funny on a sitcom, but in a real marriage it's a paper cut that won't heal. Leave the sarcastic comments that damage women and tear down marriage to other, lesser, men. While those guys are scratching their heads wondering why their wives don't want to have anything to do with them, you'll be building something beautiful on a solid foundation.

#41

Plan a Stay-at-Home Date.

 CR SO

I f you have kids, make plans for them elsewhere. Get some take-out food, a few candles, and give her a long, slow back rub. Did you know that a gentle back rub is braille for, *"I love you"* and all sorts of other intimate messages?

#42

Embrace the reality that the two of you

make up one, distinct, entity.

CR ЯО

*F*amily and friends are on the outside looking in. Be wise and seek counsel, but don't allow others from the outside to unduly influence you and to pry into your private lives before you're ready to share. You don't owe them personal information. And, if they're offended? Don't worry, they'll eventually get over it. As for the few who don't, too bad for them. No one (including family) belongs on the inside of your relationship until you've invited them there.

#43

You were made strong for a reason so, act like a man and shoulder your responsibilities.

ॐ ॐ

L ikewise, you husbands, dwell with your wives according to knowledge, giving honor unto the wife as unto the weaker vessel, and as being heirs together of the grace of life; that your prayers be not hindered. 1 Peter 3:7

#44

Take the lead.

CR RO

*W*hen it comes to dancing, only one can lead. There's one CEO of Apple, Inc., and there's only one President of the United States. Marriage is no different. Apathy is like dry rot to a marriage. You're in the position of husband, so do what good husbands do: Lead with gentleness and collaboration, but lead.

#45

Never contradict your wife in public.

രു ഇ

We've all been to the party with the couple who thinks their personal argument should command the attention of everyone in the room. Decide you're not going to be that couple and save disagreements for private conversation – away from everyone, especially the kids.

#46

It's Movie Night at home, but forget Rambo.

☙ ❧

Occasionally surprise her and pick a 'chick flick' you know she will enjoy and then shock her socks off – enjoy it with her! So chick flicks aren't your thing? Once in a while won't kill you and you might really enjoy the way the story ends at the end of the evening. WARNING: If you can't completely enter in and do this with a whole heart – if you're unable to prevent sighs, huffs, yawns, and disparaging remarks, you might want to take a pass on this one!

#47

Your anniversary matters, even if she says it isn't important.

છ જી

Just do yourself a favor and decide right now that you are going to make a BIG DEAL of your anniversary. It doesn't have to be expensive or extravagant. Setting aside a day or even a few hours to celebrate (or two nights away if you can swing it) is simply The Smart Husband's way of communicating value, love, and care. No man ever regretted cherishing his wife by celebrating "Our Anniversary".

#48

Write a love note and leave it on her pillow to find later.

CR SO

I can feel the resistance from here! So, you're not a poet? No one is suggesting you become one. But, come on! There are only about a million variations on, "*Baby, you're the BEST!*" And the simple act of buying a generic card (the kind I always get) and writing a few sincere words of what you think of your awesome woman will make her feel like a million.

#49

Holds hands.

 C ❧ ❧

When you go for a walk, a drive . . . actually, hold hands everywhere you go. Wanting to hold her hand is an easy way to whisper, *"I like being connected with you."*

#50

Keep your heart at home, even when you travel.

∞ ∞

*T*each yourself: The *best* place is at home, by her side. You are not a victim. You make the choice when faced with the many inducements to pull your heart away from what is best and highest.

No man ever made a 'snap' decision to be unfaithful. When men allow their hearts to be pulled away from the home, it's a long, incremental process, so recognize your responsibility to keep your heart desiring home.

The man with roving affections has an insecure wife, always begrudging his time away with the guys. A man whose wife knows his heart is at home will practically kick him out the door to spend time with his buddies.

#51

Pray for her.

✿ ✿

God has invited you to pray about all things. Are you praying for what He identified as one of your most important priorities?

#52

Ask her to pray for you often.

CR ⅏

*M*en typically have far more needs and concerns than they acknowledge and yet your best prayer partner – the one who knows you from the inside – is right there beside you. Mention something specific that you would like her to pray for you this week and make it a habit. Caring for each other in this way draws you closer together.

#53

Your wife's radiance - her countenance - in large measure is a reflection of how well she is loved by you.

છ ૪૭

*I*f, in your case, this is the good news then, *congratulations*! If it's the bad news, then do yourself a favor, take responsibility, and get busy adding a sparkle to her eyes by what you do and say.

#54

You don't own your body.

CR SO

Your body, including all the parts, doesn't belong to you. It belongs to your wife so it doesn't get to go places and do things she doesn't know about and wouldn't approve of. (1 Corinthians 7:4)

#55

Let her satisfy your passion.

⋐ ⋑

*T*he only people who think God is a bit of a prude –
Who frowns on sex – haven't bothered to get the facts –
some of them fairly steamy. Here's how the Bible puts it:

> *Let your fountain be blessed; and rejoice with the wife of your youth . . . . . let her breasts satisfy you at all times; and be ravished always with her love.*

> ~King Solomon, Proverbs 5:18,19

Sometimes, husbands can overlook the fact that, for wives,
physical intimacy involves a sacred giving. When something sacred is given, we should express our deep
gratitude.

#56

Choose contentment with her.

CR SO

*R*emind yourself often that you are content with this great gift God has given you. The world will scream the opposite message to you, so you've got to counteract that false voice with the Voice of Truth. Listen to only that voice and you'll build something with the strength to go the distance.

#57

Surprise her with a picnic and a stroll afterward - take care of all the details.

∞

*I*f you're like most men, this is just the kind of thing you're not great at. But, seriously, how difficult can it be? A couple of sandwiches, fruit, drinks, a blanket and napkins and you're good to go. With just a little effort, you're in the running for the '*Most Romantic Day With My Woman*' award!

#58

You've shown appreciation and that's good. Even better to help with the work around the home.

ભ્ર ∞

*I*t's vital to express gratefulness for all she does, but there's more. Yes, you work 8+ hours a day five days a week but she (especially as a young mom and/or working mother) works 24/7 so don't expect her to do it all.

#59

Helping with the vacuuming isn't a substitute for romance (for most women!).

CR SO

You are willing to help with the chores. That makes you one of the "good ones" but never let yourself believe working around the house is a substitute for romance. It might be a welcomed gesture, but helping with housework and picking up the living room isn't necessarily a stand-in for "Taking her away from it all."

CR SO

Marrying Lisa, I knew I'd hit it big. We were on our way to "epic" marriage status about four months into it. All that was necessary was *Super Husband* and he was here so we're good to go!

So why was Lisa in the kitchen with *that look* on her face?

That look ... the one that says, *"I'm not happy and YOU are the reason."*

Time to put my foot down, which always makes conversations between husbands and wives more interesting. Please forgive us, ladies. Sometimes we just can't resist, even if the result is more like stepping on something in the barnyard than clearing up the problem.

But, was that going to stop me? Ugh . . . no.

"Okay, so what's bugging you?" I said in, well, maybe not the most loving, gentle way. Which is kind of natural when you know you are the answer to the question.

She didn't answer – at least with her mouth.

The flames (the ones coming out of her eyes) and her hands did the talking as she vigorously dried the dinner plate and set it down with that decisive air you use just short of it shattering into 1,000 pieces.

Instead of breaking the plate, she shattered the silence.

"You take me for granted."

"Take you for granted . . . are you kidding me?! I'm practically Superman around here. I don't know one other guy that does the stuff I do ALL THE TIME! I help with the dishes, I help folding the clothes, I fixed the washing machine myself, I vacuum, I . . . ."

Facts are soooo helpful in moments like these. Talk about ungrateful.

It's a good thing towels don't break. She threw it on the counter and turned to face me. *"I don't care if you do ANY of those things. I just want you to take me out for coffee more than once in a blue moon. But most of all, I just want you to want to be with me."*

"But, I am with you. All the time! That plate that just survived a near death experience, I was standing next to you washing it two minutes ago! Remember?"

"That doesn't count."

"Doesn't count? Are you telling me that all my work around here to prove I care and love you counts for nothing?"

"I didn't say "nothing" but, well, they are next to nothing compared to how I feel when you want to spend time with me, away from all the stuff that has to be done."

Wow, who knew love was so easy? Just communicate that you want to be with her, that you want her – that you want to be close. Time away with her from the demands of the day communicates love to her. It's not rocket science.

Sometimes we're so busy communicating to our spouse in ways that say "love" to us, we miss that she/he might be different. What says "love" to you may not say "love" to her.

And, the best part about it, it's easy to find out what says "love" to her . . . over a cup of coffee . . . in some funky little shop she loves . . .

"Hey Gorgeous, if you had to name three things that make you feel loved by me, what would they be?"

#60

Tell her that you need her.

ଓ ଞୋ

*O*ccasionally whispering, *"I need you"* with sincerity meets a deep need in her soul. She wants to, no, she *needs to feel needed* by you – physically, yes, but also as a person who is helping you become a better man.

#61

Tell her when you need her.

CR ЕO

*B*e bold and tell her the truth. The fact is, *you need* her physically. Most guys don't want to admit they need anything because they feel instinctively that doing so communicates weakness. But it won't, not to your woman. She wants to satisfy your sexual needs and your desires. And, you *do* need her. Sex is something you were designed to need. And that's a very good thing. It was God's idea that you are made this way.

#62

Never, ever look (interestedly, longingly, lustfully) at another woman with your eyes - or with your mind.

∞ ∞

Train yourself to turn your eyes away at every opportunity that presents itself. And, don't tell yourself the convenient lie, *"I just can't help it"*. You CAN help it! Your flesh just doesn't want to.

Don't lie to yourself. If you're scouting, you are hurting your marriage by dishonoring your wife. Stay in command of your flesh and honor the woman God gave you . . . and honor the God who gave her to you. Be faithful in this area.

Every act was preceded by a thought. This is why foolish men become unfaithful. They told themselves that no harm was being done. After all, they were only *thinking* about it. It wasn't like they were actually going to *do* it.

True faithfulness – the kind that will keep you out of trouble and is approved by God - is total faithfulness. After all, the two of you are one. That includes your mind.

I will set no worthless thing before my eyes.
~ King David, Psalm 101:3

King David ignored his own advice and paid a heavy price, but you don't have to. The Bible says, *There is no temptation you face but that which is common to every man; but, God is faithful, who will not allow you to be tempted beyond what you are able to face, and will, with the temptation also provide a way of escape so you can endure it.* 1 Corinthians 10:13 (MLJ paraphrase)

God has provided the power for you to triumph in the face of temptation. Exercise that power, escape the temptation, and honor your wife.

#63

Get away together.

ଓ ଈ

*I*f at all possible (our true priorities are almost always possible) purpose to get away together for a couple of nights at least once a year.

#64

Speak words of truth, delivered with gentleness, love, and support

ଔ ଛ

A lot of guys feel they can never say anything evaluative or corrective to their wives. In many cases, that's because they ignore context, the timing, and the spirit in which it is done. Remember that old adage: *People don't care how much you know until they know how much you care?* It's especially true of our wives. Cultivate caring before you ever correct. Give careful attention to these matters before you purpose to speak. If I have something of this nature to say, I ask God to help me say it in a manner Lisa can hear and to give her the grace to hear it as it's meant.

#65

Be loyal.

ભૂ ૪૭

*A*lways take her part. She needs to know, down to her socks, that she can always count on you to have her back. Never be evaluative of her to a third party. When it comes to marriage, be a partisan, not an adjudicator. Save the evaluation for private conversation between the two of you. In public, it's always a solid, united front.

#66

Show approval with the way you look at her.

ભ્ર ৯৩

*S*he can *feel* what you're thinking and what you're feeling – whether or not you approve of her, of what she said, or is doing. Your countenance and general demeanor is important because her expert, no-fail radar is always scanning, picking up your signals.

#67

Recognize she's the weaker vessel and don't complain about it.

CR SO

From time to time, life is going to be overwhelming – that's just the way it is. Don't expect your wife to keep soldiering on with that fourth dinner party in a row, that next group of out-of-town guests, and the 15th activity that week while keeping everything else running. For the sake of order and sanity, sometimes you'll just have to say "no" or deal with these demands alone. She can do a lot but, she can't keep doing everything. Loving her means being understanding, protective, and reasonable with her limits.

#68

Make Valentine's Day irrelevant by expressions of your love all year long.

☙ ❧

Yes, you should do something for Valentine's Day (even if she's the type who says it's not important to her) but one day a year for love? Seriously? Men who truly love their wives just can't wait 364 days before expressing their love again.

#69

Tell her you'll be faithful forever.

CR ЯD

We live in a fallen world – something she knows all too well. Forget the general public, how about your average gathering of "Christians"? Divorce is more common than the cold virus. She knows you're a good man but it's encouraging and reassuring for her to hear, occasionally, that your commitment to your vow before God is as fresh in your mind as the day you uttered it.

#70

Act with kindness.

CR SO

A kind husband is a safe husband. She needs your kindness and, it's the right thing to do.

Be kind to one another, tenderhearted, forgiving one
another just as God, in Christ, has forgiven you.
~ Ephesians 4:23

#71

There is no shame in your 'Oneness' - be naked together.

ॐ ॐ

#72

Speak with grace, even (especially!) when it isn't coming back to you.

છ ૭

When she's not at her best, respond to her with the kind of grace you wish to receive when you're having "a day".

#73

Forgive with a whole heart.

જી ઓ

*S*ome forgive and never mention "it" again . . . and that's good unless they continue to harbor anger or bitterness over the incident. When you truly forgive, you let it go, move on, and enter back into full fellowship. The only other option is a root of bitterness that will eventually grow into something ugly and destructive. Let it go and refuse to take it back.

#74

Never mention today what was

forgiven yesterday.

ʘ ʘ

*E*ven in the best marriages, disagreements come, and for most, arguments happen. But there's a place you should never go when dealing with a difficulty in your relationship. If you've granted forgiveness for something, never speak of it again. It's that simple. Oh, you'll be tempted to bring up the past but don't. When we yield to our emotions and bring up something we've already forgiven, we prevent our relationship from forward progress. Remember: Forgiven means Forbidden.

#75

When you are disagreeing, stick to the issue.

ൟ ൦

When the offense is brought up, it's typical to respond with the 37 things that she did wrong. This is just pride in the way of addressing an offense. In humility, don't try to defend yourself by bringing up a single thing that she did. Just listen to the offense and respond (in the Spirit) to it. If you don't, you'll quickly discover, it wasn't worth "winning" the argument with your list of "facts". Pride makes a mess of everything it touches and what's worse, puts you in opposition to God.

God resists the proud but gives grace to the humble.

1 Peter 5:5

#76

Choose unity - cling to each other in hard times.

CR SO

*H*ard times will come. That's just what Life does —
it dishes up the hard stuff from time to time. So decide
before you enter the valley: *Nothing is going to come between
us — nothing!* And, remember, you play how you practice
so, choose unity before it gets difficult and you'll cling to
each other in the storm.

#77

Your responsibility and authority come from God, not from your personal power, so lead humbly.

ෆ ඝ

You're going to give an account of your words and deeds, and how you led. Never forget that you are accountable to God, in everything.

#78

Be exclusive and don't keep part of yourself in reserve.

☙ ❧

*L*et her know that she is the only one who is 100% on the inside with you. There's a great sense of security and strength that comes from knowing you're facing life with your soul mate. Many wives feel they are alone because their husbands rarely talk to them about what's happening in his world, what he is thinking, or feeling. This is not a personality trait. It is a choice . . . a wrong choice. You may be the silent type. That's fine for the rest of your relationships, but not for your marriage. Open up, communicate, and make sure she knows you are walking through this life together.

#79

You're the conductor on this train.

ରେ ଚ୍ଚ

*W*here are you going? Communicate your vision for what you want your marriage to represent – for who the family is becoming under your leadership. Your "people" need a vision – who you are and what you are about. What is the vision you are casting for your marriage and family? And, because you married (or are going to marry) an excellent woman, she'll have some excellent input.

#80

Choose to be happy.

ೞ ೠ

S ometimes husbands forget the massive impact they have on their families through their general attitude. What kind of spirit are you bringing to your marriage and home? No joy in life? This has far more to do with you than your circumstances or with other people. We all choose our perspective on those things God has called us to walk through. It's much easier to be joyful if you focus on how much you've received . . . how much you've been blessed. When you choose to be positive, you'll lift the spirits of everyone around you – especially your wife.

#81

Love your wife by taking precautions to protect yourself.

∝ ∾

*C*ounterfeits will always present themselves, let her know that they are nothing compared to the real thing: Her. With random offers of Internet filth in your inbox, there are countless ways to be unfaithful to your spouse without even leaving your house. Recognize it for what it is – an enticement to destroy everything of value that you've built. Put safeguards up and establish with yourself God's Standard: A "Zero Tolerance Policy". You'll maintain your self-respect, have a secure, happy wife, and best of all, the approval of God.

#82

How to handle harsh words:

CR ဆာ

*I*t's inevitable – put two sinners (even really nice ones like you and your lady) in a relationship and you will eventually find a reason to disagree . . . strongly . . . and to argue . . . which occasionally may escalate into some harsh words. And it's made all the worse because you "know" you are 100% correct and she is dead wrong! And then there were all those ridiculous, outlandish accusations: *You're not . . .! You never . . .! You always . . .!*

How does it make you feel when her words characterize you as some thoughtless, insensitive barnyard animal? Not exactly the stuff of heart-to-heart fellowship and oneness before God. At some point, and to some degree, this will happen and what will you do then? Will you allow your mind to seethe and foam on those harsh words? Or will you choose not to take offense, understanding that when her blood is up, she's capable of saying things that in her heart-of-hearts she doesn't believe are remotely true?

When we choose to walk in the flesh and become heated, we're capable of hurtful words. Don't take them to heart. They're not true, and she doesn't even believe them . . . which she will say when you both ask forgiveness and make up. Let those words go and they won't have a hold on you.

#83

Be a generous giver of second chances.

CR SD

Nothing is more natural to the flesh than to stand in judgment of another person when a genuine mistake, or wrong is committed. *You don't deserve to be forgiven* we hear as we feel the consequences of someone else's actions. But, haven't you needed grace . . . for the mistakes/bad decisions/hurtful actions you've done in the past? I'm pretty sure you don't get what you deserve, and neither do I. Be quick to offer the grace you desire when you find you've made a mistake. Truth is, you have been given second, third, fourth . . . many chances. Don't stand in judgment of your wife. Be quick to extend grace.

If you won't forgive men of their sins against you, your Father (God) will not forgive you. Matthew 6:15

#84

Whatever you plant grows ... what are you planting?

ca so

A woman never slams the door of her heart all at once. The age-old adage is 'you reap what you sow'. This is especially true in your relationship with your wife. And, we're *always planting something*. The weeds grow easily. Fruitful plants take careful planting and regular care but, when we're attentive, what a great harvest! Sow wisely with your words and deeds.

#85

You were made to initiate.

༄ ༀ

She was made to respond so make sure every day, when it comes to loving her, she never runs out of things to respond to.

#86

A woman doesn't want to lock the door of her heart, but under the right (wrong!) circumstances, over time, she will.

CR ЯD

With each repeated neglect of her heart and her needs, the door to her heart will close incrementally, bit by bit, and once it's closed, short of a miracle of God . . . forget about it, her heart is gone forever. So be wise and recognize what you do to encourage one and diminish the other.

#87

Stop making the little things important.

અ શ્

*E*ven in the best marriages, there are a variety of "little things" that can crop up in any given day – annoying little things, frustrating little things. So, it's not that these things are absent from a great marriage. The difference? That couple enjoying the great marriage has merely decided not to dwell on those things . . . to let them go – to keep them in their place. We've got to remember something very important about those little things: They just don't matter. If we focus on them, they will eventually take on destructiveness completely out of balance with their true importance. In every great marriage there are big things to address. A wise husband saves his attention for those and lets the rest go.

#88

Schedule your weekly Date Night.

ॐ ৯৩

*W*ow, that sounds boring, doesn't it? But, for most, it's necessary. If we're relying on spontaneity for our times together, our wife often finds herself competing against urgent priorities – a competition that never makes her feel good and that she often loses. Happy wives know they are a priority with their husbands. Scheduling "date night" may sound incredibly boring, but it doesn't have to be. If your commitment is scheduled (and that schedule is respected) it's a statement that nothing is more important than your time with her – a message she loves to receive.

#89

Don't expect your wife to make the arrangements for dinner out.

❧ ❦

Asking your wife to handle the details of date night once-in-a-blue-moon is fine, but don't let it become a habit. She wants you to take the initiative for these things – just like you did when you were dating, remember? It's another way to show where she ranks in your list of priorities.

#90

Come up behind her and kiss her

on the back of the neck.

೧ ೨

There are very good reasons for this but, I bet you already know them!

#91

Resist the impulse to try to change her.

CR SO

*C*hanging someone isn't your job and the effort always results in hurt feelings, at best, and often much worse. Furthermore, there are probably things about you that she feels need to change, as well. If there is something you truly would like to see changed, take your concern to God and leave it there. Changing people is His specialty.

#92

Remember your wife's birthday.

ଔ ୫ଠ

*P*ut this date on the calendar and defend it against all competing priorities. Doing something special on this day, even if it is a small but sincere gesture, is important. Everyone wants to be remembered . . . even the wives who say, "It's not important." Answer this self-deprecating statement with, "Oh YES YOU ARE!" by a sincere re-membrance once a year.

#93

Go on a Cheap Date.

CR ᖇᗝ

Pick up some drive-through ice cream (or coffee, or . . .?) and then keep driving. Tell her all the mundane details about your day and ask about hers. A "driving date" might be cheap but the message that I want to be with you is of immense value to her.

#94

Don't overreact to her mistakes.

ଔ ଓ

*C*hances are you've made a mistake or two, no? Allow that your wife may make a mistake from time to time. Give her the grace you give yourself (and want from others) when you make a mistake. She already feels badly about the consequences. No need to pile on. Did she have a fender bender, an overdraft, a _____ you fill in the blank. Love her with compassion and sympathy and with a non-condemning spirit, help her deal with the situation.

#95

Every time you walk in the door, search for her eyes and greet her with a smile.

#96

Tell her in advance what your schedule is.

❦ ❧

Don't just expect her to flex her day around errands and plans you spring on her at the last minute. It's simply the thoughtful thing to do.

#97

Ask her if there is something you can do that would "say Love" to her.

ೞ ೞ

*P*lan for this conversation. Take her to a quiet place where she can open up and ask the question with genuine sincerity. The question, itself, says so much about your desire to care for her but the follow through on her answer will draw you even closer together.

#98

Love your wife by drawing near to God.

❦ ❧

A sk God to do the necessary surgery in your life to remove those things that are not honoring to Him and to your wife. Ask Him to change you to be the husband He intended when He brought you and your wife together. If you are sincere, He will do it.

Draw near to God, and he will draw near to you.
James 4:8

#99

Keep the Biblical standard and ideal in front of you at all times.

CR ЮᎠ

*T*here is much here that will transform the marriages of men from almost any background but, for the Christian man, the standard has been established in the Word of God and, it's not optional:

> *Love your wife as Christ loves the Church and gave Himself for it.* Ephesians 5:25

This is a problem. This standard for Christian marriage is, humanly speaking, ridiculous. You can't measure up to loving your wife as Christ loves the Church and gave Himself for her, and neither can I.

Fortunately for men (and women!) there is more to the story. Galatians 2:20 says, *"I am crucified with Christ, nevertheless, I live, yet not I, but Christ lives in me."* When the life of Christ is animating what husbands do, there are a lot of wives around who are loved as Christ loves the Church and what was ridiculous becomes reality in your marriage and mine.

Yes, it's a high standard. Would we expect Jesus to establish anything less? He expects nothing less from us.

#100

Make a decision: I am going to love my wife.

ℭ ℜ ℬ

Choose to love. Always choose love. Every day, this choice presents itself many times and in many ways. If you choose to make decisions that say, "I love you," rather than those that say, "I love me", you are on your way to a great marriage.

And, one last thought:

A great marriage isn't today's destination, it's a life-long journey of two spouses learning to love richly through all the seasons of their life together. Why not get started today?

If you enjoyed and found this book practical, I'd greatly appreciate if you'd leave your review on Amazon.

About the Author

My name is Matthew L. Jacobson (feel free to call me Matt!) and I should start by telling you the best thing about me. God is so good! 21 years ago, I met and married (Saint) Lisa. You can catch up with her at her blog, Club31Women.com. We live with our eight kids on a small acreage in the Pacific Northwest – well, most of them, anyway. Our oldest is off to college on the east coast. On any given day, you can catch us in the lake, on the river, in the garden, feeding the chickens or the cow…or reading a good book by the fireplace.

For the past 23 years, I've worked in the book publishing industry as VP of Marketing & Editorial, Multnomah Press, Sr. Acquisitions Editor of Broadman & Holman, and VP of Editorial, Multnomah Publishers, founder and president of Loyal Publishing, and founder and president of Loyal Arts Literary Agency.

About eleven years ago, I started Loyal Publishing where Eric and Leslie Ludy published their bestselling book, *When God Writes Your Love Story.*

After selling Loyal Publishing (I never fit very well into the corporate world!), I began Loyal Arts Literary Agency, which represents such authors as Darlene Schacht (Time-Warp Wife), Aaron & Jennifer Smith (Unveiled-Wife) Eric & Leslie Ludy, Kevin Malarkey (*The Boy Who Came Back From Heaven* — a #7 New York Times Bestseller), Bruce Edwards, and Sheri Rose Shepherd.

Lisa and I have written several children's books including, *The Amazing Beginning of You!* , *The Big 10 for Little Saints,* and the C. S. Lewis Silver Medal winner for Children's Literature, *How Did God Make Me?*

For the past ten years, I've been a teaching elder at Tumalo Bible Fellowship, where we exalt Jesus Christ, striving to walk in open, authentic Christian fellowship and faithfulness to God through obedience to His Word.

If you'd like to check out my website, here's a sample of the articles you'll find:

For Him . . . 103 Words of Affirmation Every Husband Wants to Hear

For Her . . . 102 Words of Affirmation Every Wife Wants to Hear

For Parents . . . 7 Things Every Daughter Needs to Hear

from Her Dad and 8 Basics Every Man Should Teach His Son

You can find me on the web here:

www.MatthewLJacobson.com

Facebook: MatthewLJacobson

Twitter: @MLJacobson

See also the companion book,

100 Ways to Love Your Husband

by Lisa Jacobson.

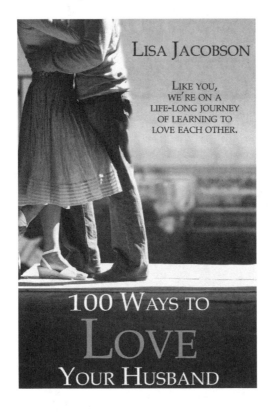

Notes & Ideas

Notes & Ideas

Notes & Ideas

Notes & Ideas

Notes & Ideas

Notes & Ideas

Notes & Ideas

Notes & Ideas

Notes & Ideas

Notes & Ideas

Notes & Ideas

Notes & Ideas

Notes & Ideas

Notes & Ideas